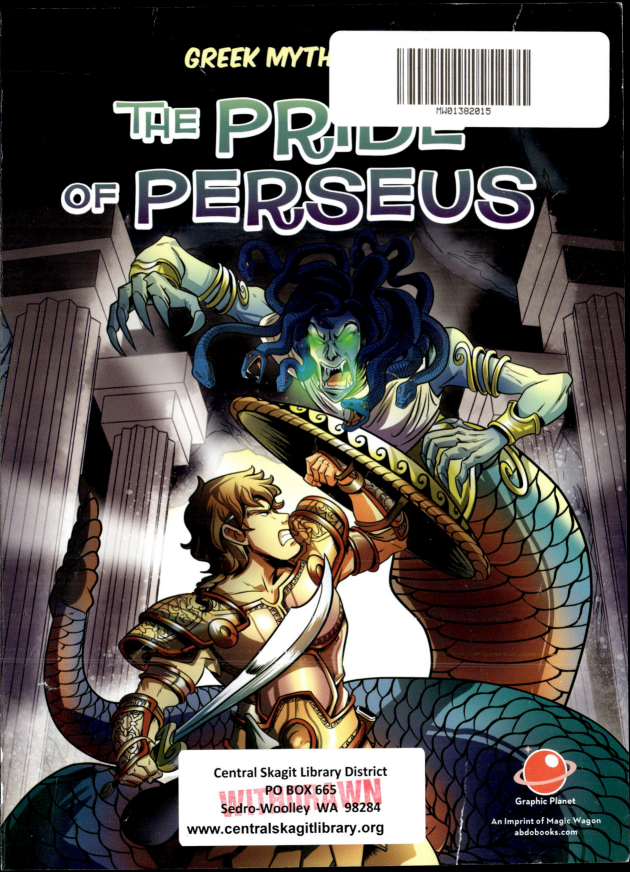

THIS BOOK IS DEDICATED TO MY CHILDREN BILL, KATHRYN, AND JASMINE, FOR WHOM I'VE TRAVELED FAR AND WIDE FOR THAT WHICH THEY'VE NEEDED AND DESIRED. -DC

TO EVERYONE WHO LOVES A GREAT GREEK STORY ESPECIALLY MY CAT MIMITO. ILLUSTRATING THIS COLLECTION WAS CHALLENGING AND FUN. I LOVED THE WHOLE PROCESS. -LA

Published by Magic Wagon, a division of ABDO, PO Box 398166, Minneapolis, Minnesota 55439. Copyright © 2022 by Abdo Consulting Group, Inc. International copyrights reserved in all countries. No part of this book may be reproduced in any form without written permission from the publisher. Graphic Planet™ is a trademark and logo of Magic Wagon.

Printed in the United States of America, North Mankato, Minnesota.
102021
012022

THIS BOOK CONTAINS RECYCLED MATERIALS

Written by David Campiti
Illustrated and Colored by Lelo Alves
Lettered by Kathryn S. Renta
Editorial Supervision by David Campiti/MJ Macedo
Packaged by Glass House Graphics
Research Assistance by Matt Simmons
Art Directed by Candice Keimig
Editorial Support by Tamara L. Britton

Library of Congress Control Number: 2021941228

Publisher's Cataloging-in-Publication Data

Names: Campiti, David, author. | Alves, Lelo, illustrator.
Title: The pride of Perseus / by David Campiti ; illustrated by Lelo Alves.
Description: Minneapolis, Minnesota : Magic Wagon, 2022. | Series: Greek mythology
Summary: Perseus slays the gorgon in a graphic novel interpretation of this classic Greek myth.
Identifiers: ISBN 9781098231835 (lib. bdg.) | ISBN 9781644946657 (pbk.) | ISBN 9781098232399 (ebook) | ISBN 9781098232672 (Read-to-Me ebook)
Subjects: LCSH: Perseus (Greek mythological character)--Juvenile fiction. | Mythology, Greek--Juvenile fiction. | Gods, Greek--Juvenile fiction. | Heroes--Juvenile fiction. | Medusa (Gorgon)--Juvenile fiction. | Adventure stories--Juvenile fiction | Graphic Novels--Juvenile fiction.
Classification: DDC 741.5--dc23

TABLE OF CONTENTS

CHARACTER GUIDE 4

THE PRIDE OF PERSEUS 5

WHAT DO YOU THINK? 30

MYSTERIES BEHIND THE MYTHS 31

GLOSSARY & ONLINE RESOURCES 32

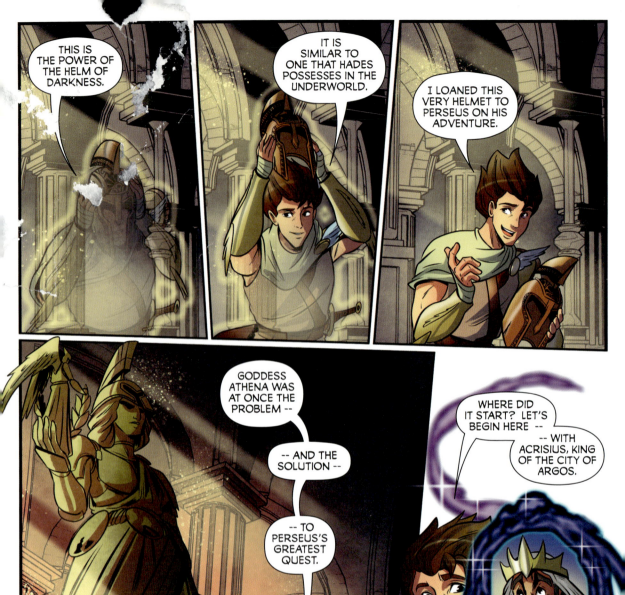

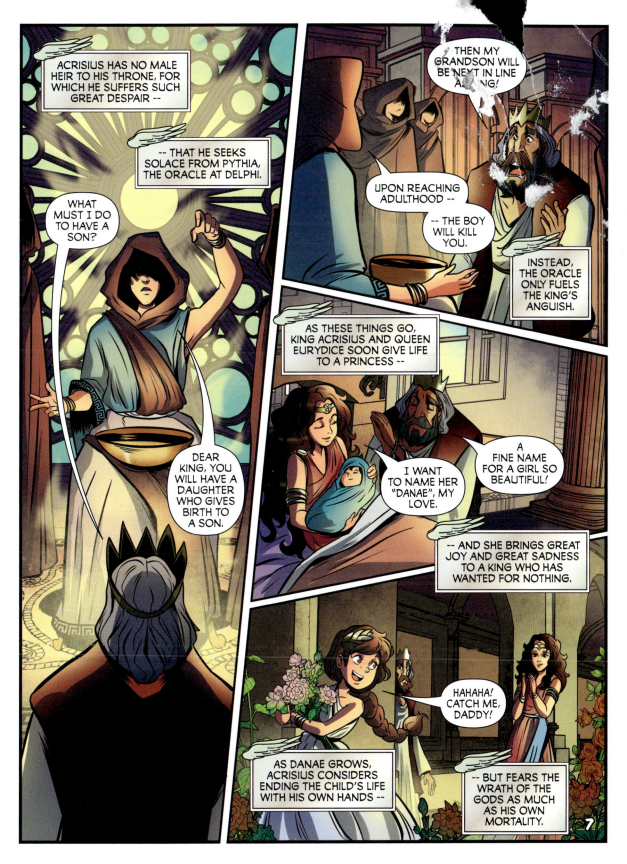

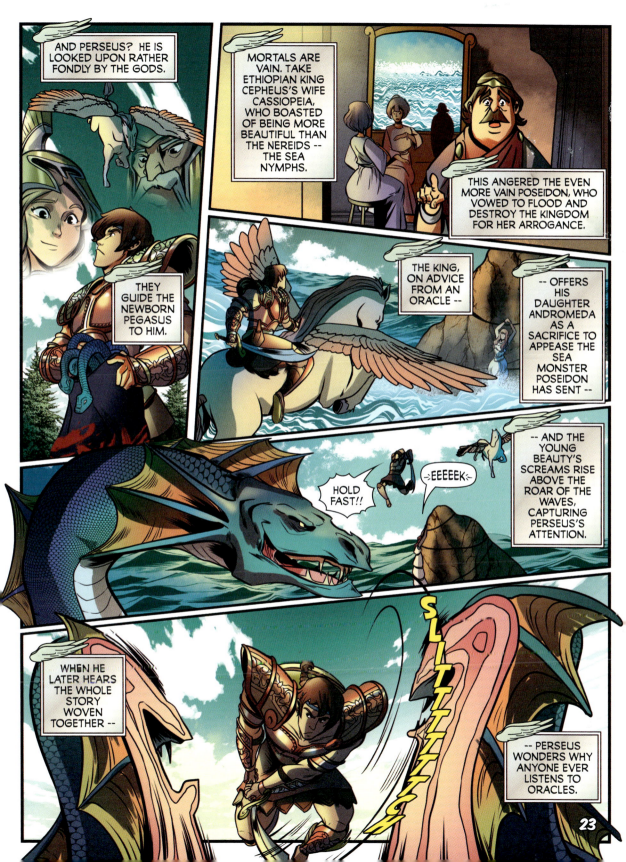

WHAT DO YOU THINK?

1. There are many myths about Perseus. In one, Perseus's adventures occur before Heracles was born, so Heracles could not have held up the cosmos for Atlas. In another, Perseus meets Acrisius and, accused of lying about beheading Medusa, Perseus turns Acrisius to stone. In still another, Dictys's wife dies, so upon becoming king he takes Danae as his Queen. What's your favorite Perseus myth? Why do you think there are so many?

2. The sea god Poseidon desired the beautiful Medusa and gave in to temptation with her in the temple of Athena. Enraged, Athena cursed Medusa, transforming her into the creature that turned mortals to stone. Was Athena right or wrong to blame Medusa? Why or why not?

3. Medusa, a mortal even as she was made into a monster, had two sisters—Stheno and Euryale. Both were immortal. What do you think happened to the sisters after Perseus killed their sister Medusa, and Pegasus and Chrysaor were born?

4. Pegasus went on to further adventures. Bellerophon, a great slayer of monsters, used Athena's charmed bridle to capture Pegasus. He mounted the flying steed and flew into battle against the Chimera. In triumph, Bellerophon rode Pegasus to Mount Olympus to join the gods. What do you think happened then?

5. According to some myths, Athena's Aegis was not a metal shield onto which Hephaestus fused Medusa's head. It was animal skin worn as extra protection. Medusa's face was removed from her skull and sewn into the animal skin to strike fear in battle. As a weapon or protection, what benefits do each version of the Aegis offer to the soldier using it?